The Magic Rainbow Hug©
A Fun Interactive Storyteller - Child Activity

JANET A. COURTNEY, PhD

D1567956

An imaginative story to help children overcome fear and anxiety through relaxation skill building, and caring and playful interactive activities.

Illustrations by:

Grace, age 8 and Benjamin, age 10

Based upon the therapeutic approach of *FirstPlay Kinesthetic Storytelling*®

(Children may know this approach as playful "BACK Stories")

*This book is dedicated to the wellbeing of children
worldwide who constantly remind us
that PLAY and Imagination are
two of life's greatest gifts*

ACKNOWLEDGMENTS

It is with the deepest of gratitude that I offer my appreciation to all the wonderful people who have helped to bring *The Magic Rainbow Hug©* to fruition. To my husband, Robert Nolan, PhD, my sons, Austin and Jesse, my daughter-in-law, Stephanie, my sister, Carol, and my mother, Margaret, whose unending support, feedback, and encouragement helped to make this book a reality ~ thank you and I love you. To my granddaughters, Sophia and Abigail, whose presence always makes me smile, sing and dance ~ I give lots of Rainbow Hugs and kisses.

I stand in awe when I view the illustrations created by Grace and Benjamin (ages 8 and 10, respectively). I am deeply thankful for your wondrous gifts of insight and playfulness that helped to create the story drawings. To Rosanne Sammis, the talented Art teacher at The Benjamin School, thank you for holding the containment for Benjamin and Grace to shine. My deepest gratitude goes to Karen Baldwin, the mother of Benjamin and Grace for all her support over the years and for showing me what great mothering really means. I am deeply appreciative for the artistic talents of Kristen Krumenacker who provided the image of the hail.

Thanks to my dear friends and colleagues for your generous gifts of time and talents: Daniela Riccelli for helping to get this project jump started; Lady Xenia Bowlby for sharing with me the Weather Massage; Linda Haase for her spot-on editing and excellent story suggestions; Pamela S. Wynn for her coaching and undertaking the technical steps of putting it all together; Karen Lester for the wonderful photos; Morgan Houck and Nancy Luellan for their valuable computer savvy; Joyce Mills for her heartfelt guidance to the storyline; Jesse Crowley for his creativity in making the video; my mentors Susan Gray, Joyce Mills, the late Viola Brody and John Heider for imparting the knowledge that makes *The Magic Rainbow Hug©* stand on solid theoretical foundation; the faculty of the School of Social Work at Barry University for advancing the field of play therapy; a big heart-hug to my closest friends~ and you know who you are~ for years of attentive listening and for reviewing the story and offering helpful suggestions.

Most importantly, I am deeply thankful to all the children and families who have practiced *FirstPlay Kinesthetic Storytelling®* (also known as, "BACK Stories™") in real-life and shared your experiences with me. Your stories touch my heart deeply. To all the child practitioners who are using the therapeutic technique of *FirstPlay Kinesthetic Storytelling®* in practice, thank you for sharing with me all of your amazing therapy successes. All I can say is WOW!

INTRODUCTION

Dear Storytellers,

The Magic Rainbow Hug© has evolved over two decades as a delightful story in my play therapy practice. It is based on *FirstPlay Kinesthetic Storytelling*® (aka: "BACK Stories™"), a therapeutic intervention that reduces fears and anxieties in children while helping them grow feelings of comfort, calm and relaxation. It is a fun, interactive adult-child (siblings too!) activity that engages children at multiple sensory levels including touch, sound, smell, sight, imagination and relaxation. The unique method for telling this children's story is through varied hand motions on a child's back that follow along with the story. Although this is always optional per the child's request—see the next page under "How to Use this Book."

The story opens with a mother telling her daughter how she learned about the magic of a *Rainbow Hug©* from her own mother. Intrigued, the little girl asks, "What's a rainbow hug? How can I get hugged by a rainbow? What will it feel like?" As a story within a story unfolds, the little girl learns how a playful puppy and two adventurous siblings discover the amazing heartfelt peace of a healing rainbow.

Since I was a young child, I have been fascinated by the natural world, from the excitement of a first snowfall, to the comfort of the sound of rain on a window pane, to the thrill of seeing a rainbow. The *Magic Rainbow Hug©* emerges from the wondrous gifts of metaphor that our changing ecology offers. The weather is used to parallel life's problems and solutions, and the rainbow ~ even since ancient times ~ symbolizes hope and renewal.

While listening to the story, children learn methods of relaxation while also enhancing receptiveness to positive caring touch. Indirect positive suggestions act to transform a child's internal perceptions of self and the world around them. Their outer life experience such as abuse, bullying, divorce, domestic violence, foster care, illness, hospitalization, loss due to death (human or pets), loss due to natural disasters (earthquakes, fire, hurricanes, tornados, tsunamis), may not change, but how they *feel* and *respond* to the problem *can* change. Herein is the HOPE.

As an American Red Cross volunteer, I adapted this story to help bring relief to children in emergency shelters affected by the 2004 Florida hurricanes. I discovered then the power of metaphoric storytelling to help soothe children suffering from the terrifying effects of natural disasters. After hearing the story, the children in the group therapy sessions were less anxious as they drew a multitude of beautiful rainbow images.

The illustrations in this book were created by two young siblings, Grace, age 8, and Benjamin, age 10, who inspired by hearing the story and feeling it on their backs, used their imaginations to create the beautifully vibrant paintings. This story can be used to help children struggling with a specific problem (see the last pages of this book) or it can be read as an entertaining story for children of all ages. I wish for you hours of spontaneous fun as you and your child share this distinctive form of storytelling.

With Warm Regards,

Janet A. Courtney, PhD

Parent Websites:

Visit: FirstPlayCafe.com

Visit: Magicrainbowhug.com

For Practitioner Training:

Visit: FirstPlayTherapy.com

How to Use this Book

Like any children's story, it can be read to capture your child's imagination. However, the intent of this book is to teach you how to use this story as a playful activity drawn on your child's back with your fingers. Each activity includes instructions, located in brackets on the bottom of each page, on how to perform each technique. As your child is listening to the story they are engaging their imagination while at the same time connecting to an awareness of sensation by also *feeling* the story.

Research has shown that touch can help reduce stress in children while also increasing levels of empathy and parent-child bonding. When we give caring touch, the feel-good "love" hormone oxytocin is released, and instantaneously the stress hormone, cortisol, is decreased. Children have varied touch sensitivities. Therefore adjust the amount of touch from light to firm pressure.

Positive suggestions are in italics and interspersed throughout the story. When you read these words ~ change your tone to make it livelier, slower, quieter or louder. Your vocal variety entices your child to listen more intently. Some of the instructions suggest you participate in the relaxation methods with your child. For example, the instructions may indicate for you to also take a breath and breathe out, or to sing a sound such as "Ahhhhhhh." Your modeling of the relaxation method helps to increase your child's eagerness to practice while also increasing a level of mutual attunement.

The Magic Rainbow Hug© is more than just a metaphoric story. It is also about skill building. Once you have learned the basics of the hand movements, you can adapt this story to meet the needs of your child. For instance, your child may have a favorite animal, such as a kitten, that can be sketched as the main character. This enhances your child's own connection and enthusiasm to the story as their imagination is engaged to further embellish the storyline.

Before you begin, always ask permission first from your child prior to engaging in any of the activities. You can do this by simply saying, "Hey, would you like for me to tell you a "BACK Story™" (or a "HAND Story™")? This sends a powerful message to your child that he or she is respected. Know that the interactive part is always optional and your child can just listen to the story if desired. All is good!

The Magic Rainbow Hug©

Outside the rain is falling softly as a little girl is getting ready for bedtime. "Mommy, tell me a story," she says.

Her mother replies, "Tonight I am going to tell you a very special story that my mother told me and her mother told her. It's a very different kind of story because it is a story I can also tell you by drawing it on your back."

The little girl wonders, "Really? A story that I can *imagine* AND *feel*?"

Her mother smiles and nods her head, "Yes, that's right."

"What's the story about?" asks the little girl.

Her mother answers, "It's a story about a sweet little girl named, Sophie, her fun-loving brother, Jesse, their lovable puppy, Oscar, and how they discovered the healing magic of a *Rainbow Hug.*"

"A Rainbow Hug? What's a Rainbow Hug? How can I get hugged by a rainbow? What will it feel like?" asks the little girl.

The mother says tenderly, "By the end of the story you will *discover the answers* to all those questions. But before I begin, we need to get ready for this exciting new adventure…"

She asks the little girl to sit in front of her, and then the mother gently brushes off the little girl's back and shoulders.

Clearing Path
Have the child sit in front of you with his/her back turned toward you, and then lightly brush the shoulders and back.

The mother says, "OK, now we are ready to begin the story…"

It is a bright sunny day at Imagination Park. Sophie and Jesse are happily running, skipping, and jumping all around having fun teaching their playful puppy Oscar some new tricks.

Sophie throws the ball and says, "Here Oscar catch this."

Oscar leaps up and catches the ball. He's having so much fun since Sophie and Jesse adopted him from the *Hope Street Animal Shelter.*

Figure Outline
Draw an outline of a girl, a boy, and a puppy on the child's back (stick figures work best).

Playing Action
Next, with both hands, move your fingers all around as if the children and puppy are happily playing together.

Sophie and Jesse stretch their arms wide open and *enjoy the warm touch* of the earth's magnificent sun.

The sun's rays of light radiate out in all directions ~ some go up ~ some go down ~ and some go to the sides.

Sun

Make your hand into a fist and slowly make three circular rotations clockwise on the upper middle part of the back.

Next, use your fist to draw "rays" of light moving out in all different directions.

Even Oscar loves to soak up the sunshine. He rolls over and Sophie and Jesse rub his soft, furry belly. They watch in amazement as Oscar's body *relaxes* and goes limp.

Jesse says, "I think having his belly rubbed must be Oscar's favorite thing in the whole wide world."

Running

Using both hands, lightly move your fingers quickly around at different spots on the child's back.

Just then they see a huge shadow fall across the ground. Sophie, Jesse and Oscar look up toward the blue sky and see some dark clouds rolling in.

Sophie says, "The sun is beginning to hide behind the clouds."

Jesse wonders, "Hmmm…It looks like it's going to rain. Where can we go?"

Clouds

With your fingers, first draw the outline of at least three clouds on the upper part of the child's back and then with your fist "color in" the clouds.

Sophie, Jesse and Oscar look around, and to their surprise they see a colorful stone castle up on the hill. They *know* immediately that it's *just the right place* to go.

Sophie exclaims, "Oh, a beautiful castle. Let's go there."

Jesse says, "Perfect! Let's follow that path."

They run into the castle where a friendly sign greets them:

Welcome to Imagination Park's
Safe Place Storm Shelter

Shelter

Draw an outline of a castle (or another type shelter of the child's choosing) on the upper back.

Running to "Safe Place"

Emphasize the words *safe place* as you run your fingers across the back into the imagined shelter. Next, place one hand flat against the back for 3 seconds to provide a feeling of support and safety.

From a *comfortable place inside* the *protective* castle, they watch from a window as the trees begin to sway in the wind. The wind blows stronger…and… stronger…and then… faster… and faster. It's almost as fast as a loop-de-loop roller coaster at a fun amusement park.

Wind

Sweep your hand from side to side, first with your palm flat from right to left, then, turn your hand over and sweep across the child's back from left to right.

Start slowly and then increase the speed and pressure as you move your hand faster and faster back and forth.

Sophie says, "It's starting to rain. That must make all the thirsty plants and flowers really happy."

They *listen* as the rain drizzles down softly, *gently touching* the pretty flowers.

Gradually, the rain gets louder and louder and louder, and then to their total amazement, it turns into ice.

The icy little balls make a plop, plop, plop, sound as they bounce all over the ground.

Jesse shouts, "Look, Sophie, that's hail!"

Rain

With both hands, begin at the shoulder and stroke downward with your fingertips. Continue to stroke downward faster and faster.

Hail

With your fingertips, draw round balls of hail while lightly bouncing your fingers as you move to different spots on the child's back.

Suddenly, the whole sky glows as lightning flashes behind the fluffy clouds. And then they *hear* the rumbling and crackling sound of thunder. Ka-BOOM, ka-BOOM, ka-BOOM! BOOM! BOOM!

Seeing the worried look on Oscar's face, Sophie pats his head and says, "It's okay Oscar, it's just like the exciting fireworks of a holiday celebration."

While little Oscar nestles between them *for comfort*, Sophie and Jesse *relax* by making their own sound. They take a long ~ deep ~ *calming ~ breath* and sing, "Ahhhhhhh, ahhhhhhh, ahhhhhhh..."

Lightning

With one hand, form a fist and make long zigzag motions starting at the top of the shoulder and moving back and forth across the spine to the bottom.

Thunder

Using both hands, take your fists and lightly beat across the top of the shoulders and upper back taking care not to hit the spine. Adjust touch as needed.

Relaxed Breath

While doing the thunder, have the child take a deep breath and while exhaling sing, "Ahhhhhhh." Join in this sound holding the exhale 5-10 seconds. Repeat.

"Look at that Oscar," Sophie says, putting Oscar's nose to the window.

They see colorful leaves swirl from the ground up, up, up to the sky…twirling and whirling turning round and round.

Soon, the swirling *settles down* and the leaves come to a *gentle, relaxed rest*.

…But their adventure isn't over…

Swirling Leaves

Start at the base of the spine and make small clockwise, circular swirling motions moving up the spine. Repeat three times. On the third rotation, move your hand more slowly, then rest your hand flat in the middle of the back, imitating leaves settling down and coming to a gentle rest.

Once again the wind becomes *strong*…and with *all of its strength* it blows the last of the dark clouds away.

Sophie and Jesse *imagine* they can blow away the dark clouds. They take deep, deep, deep, long *breaths* and then blow, blow, blow all the air out of their mouths.

Jesse gets excited, "Sophie, *listen* to the sound of my *breath*. It reminds me of the ocean."

Sophie *listens closely* as Jesse breathes in ~ and ~ out, and ~ in ~ and ~ out. She replies, "Yes. It's kind of like the sound a shell makes when I hold it to my ear."

They play a fun game to see who can blow-their-breaths-out-the-longest and even pretend they are blowing bubbles.

Clouds Blowing Away

Take your hands and sweep across the child's back from right to left three times. Have the child imagine blowing all of the dark clouds away.

Breathing Activity

Along with the child, take three deep long breaths, inhaling and exhaling through your mouths. Pretend you are blowing bubbles. Play a fun game of "Who-can-blow-out-the-breath-the-longest."

"The storm is over," they shout. "Let's go back outside." They run out of the castle and *dance* in the sunshine. As they wiggle their bodies they begin to notice something around them has *changed*.

Everything feels *still* and *calm*...the air smells *sweet* and *fresh*.

Jesse says, "I can almost taste the air; it smells so yummy."

Sophie closes her eyes and sniffs the air and says, "Yes, it smells like...like...strawberry ice cream! And...and peaches! And wildflower honey! Mmmm...delicious."

Walking

Walk your fingers along the child's back representing the children and puppy exiting the castle.

Sun

With a fist, draw the sun in the middle of the back with the rays of light moving out in all different directions.

Sophie, Jesse and Oscar are amazed as a *beautiful* rainbow suddenly appears.

Jesse says, "Wow! Look at that! The rainbow stretches all the way across the sky."

It is the most spectacular, incredible, brilliant, colorful and awesome rainbow they have ever seen!

Sophie and Jesse start to name the colors ~ red, orange, yellow, green, blue, purple, violet and lots more…

Rainbow

To draw the rainbow, use your fist to make long sweeping half circles across the child's back beginning on the left side below the shoulder blades to the opposite side of the back.

Engage the child in the naming of the colors. Use the sweeping motion for each color as you say the name of the color.

Sophie's eyes widen with excitement. "Let's imagine all of those beautiful colors melting inside of us."

Just like popcorn popping in a popper, Jesse begins jumping up and down with delight. "Sophie, that's the best idea ever! ...Here, let's try this… Put your hands on your heart, and then...get really, really still."

Together, Sophie and Jesse grow very quiet, and place their hands over their hearts as little Oscar snuggles close.

In a soft slow voice, Jesse continues, "Now close your eyes ~ take a deep breath ~ and picture a beautiful rainbow."

At that moment, Sophie and Jesse *giggle* as they imagine and *feel* all of the wonderful rainbow colors flowing into their bodies, and spreading from the tippy top of their heads all the way down to their toes.

Melting Rainbow

Using both hands with palms flat, make wide figure eight motions across the back moving down from the shoulders to the bottom of the back.

They *laugh* as they feel the *tingle* of the rainbow move to their head, forehead, ears, eyebrows, eyes, nose, cheeks, mouths, chins, necks, shoulders, arms, elbows, hands, fingers, knees, calves, ankles, feet, all the way to their itsy bitsy pinky toes.

Best of all, Sophie, Jesse and Oscar have an amazing feeling of *peace, happiness* and *love* as the rainbow fills their heart.

Jesse smiles and says, " It feels like I was just *hugged* by a rainbow!"

Sophie thinks for a second, "It felt just like a…a…*RAINBOW HUG*!"

Guiding the Rainbow

Have the child imagine all the rainbow colors flowing throughout the body. You can help guide this activity. For example, start by having the child touch the top of the head and ask him/her, "What color goes to your head?" Continue with the forehead, ears, eyes, eyebrows, nose, cheeks, mouth, chin, neck, shoulders, arms, elbows, hands, each finger, knees, calves, ankles, feet and each toe. Last, have the child place the hands on his/her heart and ask what colors fill the heart.

When the mother finishes telling the story, she opens her arms wide and wraps them around her little girl. And then with *all of her love* she gives her little girl a great big, snuggly hug.

At that very moment, the little girl feels her heart swell with a wonderful feeling of *love* and *joy*.

"Your grandmother called this a *RAINBOW HUG,*" says the mother.

"Rainbow Hugs feel so good, Mommy. Can I have one every day?" asks the little girl.

The mother smiles and says, "Of course you can, every day! And just like Sophie and Jesse you can also give yourself a magic Rainbow Hug whenever you need it to be with you. All you have to do is place your hands on your heart, get really, really still, close your eyes, take a deep breath, and imagine a beautiful rainbow flowing throughout your whole body."

Learning the Rainbow Hug

Then as the mother tucks her little girl in bed, the child reaches up and *with all of her love* she gives her mother a great big, snuggly hug and whispers in her mother's ear, "Now I can give you a *Rainbow Hug* too!"

Rainbow Hug

Give a nice big warm love-hug to the child and tell them that it is a *Rainbow Hug.* Emphasize that they can also give themselves a *Rainbow Hug* by placing both hands on the heart, and becoming very still; then closing the eyes, taking a deep breath, and imagining a beautiful rainbow flowing throughout the whole body.

The Magic Rainbow Hug©

Story by, Janet A. Courtney, PhD

(A quick story version—please copy for your personal use as needed)

There once was a little _____ *(Girl; Boy; Cat; Dog; Favorite animal of child, etc.);*
and she/he *(use the same gender as the child)* was outside playing.

> DRAW AN OUTLINE: *Person or animal on the back of the child.*

It was a beautiful day and the sun that warms and lights the whole world was shining bright
in the sky. The rays of the sun shone out in all different directions—some go up, down and to the sides.

> SUN: *With a fist, make a circle on the middle back; then draw "rays" out in all directions.*

The little *(say character)* was having fun laughing, running, skipping, and jumping around.

> RUNNING: *Move your fingers around on the back as if the child or animal was playing.*

But then the little *(say character)* looked up in the sky and saw some dark clouds rolling in.

> CLOUDS: *With two fingers make an outline of three clouds on the upper back.*

So the little _____ *(say character)* looked to the side and saw a beautiful safe place to go.
It was a _____ *(castle; house; tent; name whatever the child would like)* and they ran into
the safe place and they were all *safe* and *protected inside.*

> SHELTER: *Draw an outline of the shelter with your finger and then run your fingers across*
>
> *the back   into the shelter. Emphasize the words safe and protected.*

They watched from a window as the wind began to blow. It blew faster…and faster…
and faster…

> WIND: *Move your hand from side to side first with the flat palm and then with the*
> *back of your hand.*

….Until it began to rain.

> RAIN: *With both hands begin at the shoulders and stroke downward with your finger pads. .*

Then it rained stronger and stronger until it turned to hail.

> HAIL: *Use your fingertips and playfully bounce up and down at different spots on the back.*

Then the lightening came.

>   LIGHTENING: *Take your fists and make long zig-zags motions starting at the top of the shoulder and moving back and forth across the spine to the bottom of their back.*

Then it began to thunder.

>   THUNDER: *Take your fists and lightly pound across the shoulder top and down the sides of the back taking care not to hit the spine. Adjust your touch to the needs of the child. Most children—and adults like this part. *At this point I try to have the child use sound on the exhale like an Ahhhhhh…Make the sounds with them too.*

Then the leaves started to swirl. They begin on the ground and move, up, Up, and UP to the sky. And, it happened again—they blew up, UP, UP to the sky. Swirling and twirling all around. And, once again, up, UP, UP, swirling and twirling.

>   SWIRLING LEAVES: *Start at the base of the spine and using your fist make circular swirling motions moving up the spine to the top. Repeat this three times.*

Then all of a sudden a strong wind comes and blows all…those….dark….clouds… away.

>   CLOUDS BLOWING AWAY: *Take your hands and sweep across the child's back from right to left. Have the child take a deep breath and pretend they are blowing all of the dark clouds away.*

Then the sun came out again and shone bright again in the sky.

>   SUN: *With a fist, make a circle on the middle back; then draw "rays" out in all directions.*

Then the little _____ (name character) ran out to play. Next, (he/she) looked up into the sky and saw a beautiful Rainbow suddenly appear. The rainbow had the colors of green, blue, yellow, purple, red, and more…

RAINBOW: *At this point engage the child in the naming of the colors. Use your fists to make long sweeping half circles across the back beginning below the shoulder blades to the opposite side of the back. Do the sweeping motion for each color and say the name of the color out loud.*

Then something very special happened. The little _____ (name character) looked up toward the sky, and the sparkling rainbow began to melt all over his/her body. All those beautiful colors flowed to every single part of his/her body.

MELTING RAINBOW: *Engage the child in naming where all the colors go and have the child place his or her hands on the spots. Some examples are the top of the head; the face (forehead, nose, eye brows, ears, mouth, checks), the throat, shoulders, arms, elbows, hands, each finger, palms, knees, feet and each toe.* The last place the beautiful rainbow flowed was to (his/her) heart. *Have the child place both of their hands over the heart.*

Storytellers Who Will Find this Story Helpful

- *Parents* can use *The Magic Rainbow Hug©* with their children to help decrease fear and anxiety while increasing the joy and playfulness of their relationship.
- *Grandparents* can use this with their grandchildren as a way to connect and bring more fun into their relationship.
- *Foster parents* may be able to help build an attachment relationship with a child who enters their home.
- *Psychotherapists* and *psychologists* who work with children can incorporate *The Magic Rainbow Hug©* as an adjunctive to other therapeutic interventions. When working in family therapy, practitioners can help to guide a therapist-parent-child led session.
- *School teachers*, *school counselors* and *staff* who can't touch children due to policy mandates can teach students *The Magic Rainbow Hug©* to practice with each other as a way to enhance peer-to-peer relationships.
- *Child-Care practitioners* who care for young children.
- *Massage Therapists* can use this with young children.
- *Medical Personnel* can use *The Magic Rainbow Hug©* to help ease a child's hospitalization.
- *Pediatric Occupational Therapists* can use *The Magic Rainbow Hug©* as an additional intervention when working with children diagnosed with sensory integration disorders.
- *Speech Therapists* can use this activity as a playful intervention to help emphasize articulation of speech.
- *Geriatric practitioners* can vary *The Magic Rainbow Hug©* in a non- patronizing way to initiate essential touch with the elderly.
- *Disaster relief practitioners* can use *The Magic Rainbow Hug©* to help desensitize children from the trauma caused by natural disasters.
- Those who work with *special needs populations* including children with physical disabilities or children diagnosed with autism spectrum disorders.

The Benefits of *The Magic Rainbow Hug©*

- Instills seed thoughts of Hope
- Increases an internal sense of safety and protection
- Enhances the parent-child attachment
- Intersperses messages that provide positive suggestions to create change
- Gives essential positive and nurturing touch
- Reduces fear and anxiety
- Helps to lift depression
- Heightens auditory, kinesthetic, olfactory, and visual awareness
- Increases relationship playfulness
- Encourages the use of imagination
- Induces relaxation
- Teaches children new ways of coping and alleviating stress
- Enhances awareness of one's bodily self
- Strengthens a connection to nature
- Spreads Joy, Happiness and Peace
- Enhances self-esteem
- Helps to refocus attention
- Encourages an internal sense of introspection
- Brain research has shown that joyful play promotes healthy neurological pathways

The *Magic Rainbow Hug©* can Help Children Experiencing

- Abuse, Neglect & Abandonment
- Anxiety and Fear
- Attention-Deficit/Hyperactivity Disorder
- Autistic Spectrum Disorder
- Bullying
- Depression
- Divorce
- Domestic Violence
- Foster Care
- Illness
- Hospitalization
- Learning Disorders
- Loss due to death (human or pets)
- Loss due to natural disasters (earthquakes, fire, hurricanes, tornados, tsunamis)
- Selective Mutism
- Obsessive Compulsive Disorder
- Oppositional Defiant Disorder
- Reactive Attachment Disorder
- Separation Anxiety Disorder
- Visual impairment or Blindness

About the Author

Janet A. Courtney, PhD is Founder of FirstPlay® Therapy and also The First-PLay® Café an e-magazine* for parents. She is Director of Developmental Play & Attachment Therapies, Inc. in Palm Beach County, FL specializing in expressive Play Therapies with children and families. She is author and co-editor of the groundbreaking book, *Touch in Child Counseling and Play Therapy: An Ethical and Clinical Guide* and is a Registered Play Therapy Supervisor and Chair of the Ethics and Practice Committee for the Association for Play Therapy. She is past president of the Florida Association for Play Therapy and an Adjunct Professor at the Barry University School of Social Work, Miami Shores, FL. She is a contributing author for her chapter, *Touching Autism through Developmental Play Therapy* in the book, "Play-based Interventions for Children and Adolescents with Autism Spectrum Disorders," and her research in Developmental Play Therapy, Attachment Theory, and Touch is published in the *American Journal of Art Therapy* and the *International Journal of Play Therapy*. Janet believes that children's lives are profoundly enriched through contact with nature, caring touch, and the power of imaginative storytelling. She provides keynotes and trainings worldwide and has spoken nationally and internationally in the Cayman Islands, England, Ireland, Morocco, Russia and the Ukraine. She shares about her new process of *FirstPlay Kinesthetic Storytelling®* ("BACK Stories™") in her TEDx Talk, *The Curative Touch of a Magic Rainbow Hug* (YouTube).

Dr. Courtney offers a Practitioner Certification in FirstPlay® Therapy (FirstPlay® Infant Story-Massage (ages birth to 36 months) and FirstPlay Kinesthetic Storytelling® ages two years and above). For more information, visit her website: **FirstPlayTherapy.com**

*Parents, check out the FirstPlay® Café, a unique parenting e-magazine for parents with children ages womb to six years at: **FirstPlayCafe.com**

"Hi. My name is Benjamin. I love painting watercolors, and I think it is a lot of fun. The challenging part about painting is having patience. My future goals are to become a computer designer and a great singer."

"Hi, I am Grace. I love art and math and being creative in my life. I enjoyed using my creativity in the paintings for the story, and I like thinking out of the box. One of my goals in life is to find ways to help others, not just myself."

51028198R00031

Made in the USA
Lexington, KY
30 August 2019